MW00856129

# A BRIEF HISTORY ON THE BLACK DEATH

The Black Plague Unveiled: A Compelling Collection of
Facts & Trivia From History's Darkest Pandemic

SCOTT MATTHEWS

Copyright © 2023 Scott Matthews

All rights reserved. No part of this publication may be reproduced, distributed or transmitted in any form or by any means, including photocopying, recording, or other electronic or mechanical methods, without the prior written permission of the publisher, except in the case of brief quotations embodied in critical reviews and certain other non-commercial uses permitted by copyright law.

Trademarked names appear throughout this book. Rather than use a trademark symbol with every occurrence of a trademarked name, names are used in an editorial fashion, with no intention of infringement of the respective owner's trademark. The information in this book is distributed on an "as is" basis, without warranty. Although every precaution has been taken in the preparation of this work, neither the author nor the publisher shall have any liability to any person or entity with respect to any loss or damage caused or alleged to be caused directly or indirectly by the information contained in this book.

*The more that you read, the more things you will know. The more you learn, the more places you'll go. - Dr. Seuss*

## About The Author

 Scott Matthews is a geologist, world traveller and author of the "Amazing World Facts" series! He was born in Brooklyn, New York, by immigrant parents from Ukraine but grew up in North Carolina. Scott studied at Duke University where he graduated with a degree in Geology and History.

His studies allowed him to travel the globe where he saw and learned amazing trivial knowledge with his many encounters. With the vast amount of interesting information he accumulated, he created his best selling books "Random, Interesting & Fun Facts You Need To Know."

He hopes this book will provide you with hours of fun, knowledge, entertainment and laughter.

## BONUS!

Thanks for supporting me and purchasing this book! I'd like to send you some freebies. They include:

- The digital version of *500 World War I & II Facts*

- The digital version of *101 Idioms and Phrases*

- The audiobook for my best seller *1144 Random Facts*

Go to the last page of the book and scan the QR code. Enter your email and I'll send you all the files. Happy reading!

# Contents

# 1. Introduction

## What is the Black Plague?

The year is 1346. You and your family have survived many hardships over the past few decades. You can recall the hardships of 1315, when winter seemed to be colder than ever before. You recall the famine that came after, the crops all killed by the harsh conditions. For a moment, you believe that perhaps the hardships are over. Then, your child develops an inflamed lymph node (a small bean-shaped structure that is part of the body's immune system).

For many families during this time period, this lone symptom was the first to indicate the struggles that were to come. The Black Plague, transmitted by the bites of fleas, reached pandemic levels in the year 1346, with the plague not ending until the year 1353. During this time, the continents of Europe, Asia, and North Africa would all fall victim to the disease, killing numerous people and permanently changing society.

The Black Plague is a disease that caused one of the deadliest pandemics in human history. The disease is caused by the bacteria *Yersinia pestis*, and was not uncommon prior to the pandemic of 1346. However, for reasons that scientists still speculate about, the disease began to spread quickly in that year and soon reached pandemic levels. There are three variants of the plague: pneumonic, septicemic, and bubonic. All three variants spread during the events of the Black Death, which is the official title of the pandemic of 1346.

While the initial outbreak waned a short seven years later, the plague never fully went away. While today the disease is rare, there are still cases in various parts of the world. Most cases today do not end in death, as modern medicine can now treat the disease. These treatments were not available during the initial outbreaks, however. Thus, the plague is remembered as a time of fear, death, and decay.

## Historical Context of the Black Plague

The Black Death began in 1346 and ended in 1353, shortly after killing one-third of Europe and twenty-million individuals in Asia. This took place during the Late Middle Ages, shortly after the Little Ice Age and the Great Famine. These events marked the end of a prosperous time in Europe and left the public tired and afraid. Later, this would be referred to as "The Crises of the Late Middle Ages."

The European population was reduced to half of its original numbers, leading to a populace that was no longer complacent to continue living in the feudal culture of Europe. Warfare—both civil and between other countries—plagued the continent for years afterwards. People were confused and afraid of the Black Death, a disease that would not be fully understood until centuries later. It is remembered as a time filled with medical treatments that were little more than symbolic play and a time where life and death met daily.

Bodies littered the streets and the stench of decay covered even those who were living. The number of laborers in Europe drastically decreased, leading to a labor shortage that would add to the calamity. Individuals were often forced to bury their family and governments buried the unclaimed bodies in giant pits that acted as mass graves. The disease stole the lives of many and the limbs of others.

Governments across Europe, Asia, and Africa tried to find ways to keep trade alive as the population struggled to survive. Unaware of the concept of germs, many groups of people were passively and actively blamed for the deadly plague. The lower class and foreigners were treated poorly in comparison to the wealthy. Certain ethnic groups, especially Jews, were directly accused of causing the event. Individuals that belonged to these populations died at a much higher rate than others, leading to a slow decline in morale amongst them.

The original plague ended seven years after it started, but the disease continued to cause occasional outbreaks and pandemics for centuries after. It is in these later pandemics that the concept of the plague doctor gains notoriety. The masked individual, usually poorly trained in the basic medicine of the time, would try a variety of folkloric remedies on plague-infected individuals. Their only protection was their outlandish outfits that covered the entirety of their bodies, and the special blend of herbs and perfumes stuffed into the beak of their birdlike masks.

It is also during these later pandemics that quarantine was attempted. Entire villages chose to isolate at times. In other instances, individuals would be locked into their own homes. In particularly frightening situations, people would be forced into special asylums if they were infected with the disease. Here, they were left to die.

The human race remembers the initial plague of the Black Death—and the plagues closely following it—in horror. While the disease that caused the plague can still be found in our modern society, it is now merely one of many treatable ailments. However, the legacy and sinister memories of the early "pestilence" still linger and cast a dark shadow over humankind.

## 2. The Origins of the Black Plague

### Theories on its Origins

When the plague began, medical science was in its infancy. Society was overall religious and superstitious, leading to several theories that were wildly incorrect. This led to treatments that were ineffective and even dangerous at time.

One common theory that circulated during the pandemic was that the plague was simply an act of God. Although this sentiment has been shared during modern pandemics, the version that was believed during the Black Plague excluded all discussions of science, instead believing God was directly inflicting the maladies on the populace.

Faithful Christians who caught the plague were sometimes confused as to why they were being punished, leading them to attempt to find remedies using the Bible. These failed attempts at cures led to the Christian populace further questioning the intentions of God and the church. Meanwhile, Muslims in Asia and North Africa viewed the pandemic as an act of God, but instead saw it as a gift, believing faithful Muslims who died from the plague were simply being transported directly to paradise via martyrdom.

Antisemitism and xenophobia also created some of the early theories surrounding the mysterious plague. Some individuals did not believe in a supernatural cause at all, but instead believed in a purposeful, malicious plot. While the church at the time claimed to be protective of Jewish populations, its followers were often antisemitic. Some religious individuals, instead of believing God caused the plague, decided that the Jews in their communities were to blame for the mysterious deaths and illnesses popping up.

While the exact manner in which the Jews were supposedly causing the plague differed from town to town, the most common accusation was that of poisoning. The Christians believed the Jews were poisoning the water in the community well, as many followers of Judaism did not use the municipal water source. Several attacks and massacres took place during this time, and Jews were often forced to confess to acts of poisoning that never actually took place.

Astrological happenings were also not free from blame during the pandemic. A common idea surrounding the Black Death was that it was caused by the planets, specifically Saturn, Jupiter, and Mars. Early scholars at the University of Paris claimed that these planets were in the 40th degree of Aquarius, leading to the events of the plague. Some scholars stated that the joining of Saturn and Jupiter would lead to ruin, while other claimed it was Mars and Jupiter. Some claimed that Jupiter alone was responsible, as it is a planet that is "hot and wet" according to astrology, which brings about putrefying conditions.

The final early theory that was commonly believed includes the belief in a substance called "miasma." During medieval times, some individuals believed that bad air caused all disease. This air was called a variety of names including miasma, night air, and noxious air. The air was produced when organic material rotted or when earthquakes caused dangerous gasses to be released from underground. Humans would inhale the air and it would infect the heart, which is the part of the body medieval scholars believed was responsible for the process of breathing.

Miasma theory is the theory closest to our modern understanding of disease. While technically it is not bad air that causes most diseases, the germs spread through inhalation are often the cause. It is likely that inhaling the air from a room that housed a sick person or inhaling air in a city street near a sick person could have led to certain cases of the plague, especially the pneumonic variant. Yet, this is only true when discussing the spread of the plague, not the creation.

Ultimately, the truth behind the origin of the plague lies in a common pest. Modern scientists have traced the initial infections of Yersinia pestis back to fleas. It is now believed that black rats traveled alongside raiders and traders, bringing infected fleas along with them. The rats acted unpredictably when ill with disease, leading to more contact with human populations. The disease spread quickly as the climate warmed after the events of the Little Ice Age.

The Little Ice Age was a period of cooling that occurred between the 14th and 19th centuries, primarily affecting Europe. It was characterized by a drop in average global temperatures, resulting in colder winters, shorter growing seasons, and changes in weather patterns. The cooling was likely caused by various factors, including decreased solar activity, volcanic eruptions, and changes in oceanic circulation.

This began causing the initial infections, which were traced back to Mongolia in the 1330's. Eventually, through trade and sieges from the Mongols, the disease was introduced to Europe and began to spread. This information was confirmed as being likely via finding traces of the Yersinia pestis bacteria in the teeth of plague victims.

However, scientists are still proposing alternative theories. Many claim that plague cases peaked during times when fleas are not able to reproduce and spread disease. Supposedly, the temperatures during these times would have likely been too high to allow for long-term survival of the disease. Some proposed that anthrax (a serious infectious disease caused by a rod-shaped bacteria) may be the actual cause of the pandemic. However, modern scientists refute this claim based on the concept that the medieval version of Yersinia pestis and the modern version of the disease are different. DNA testing shows that the version of the bacteria that caused the plague is not the same version that currently exists. It is believed that this earlier version of the bacteria may have been able to handle higher temperatures and may have been able to spread rapidly from a single host.

While no theory is officially confirmed, the Yersinia pestis theory is the most widely accepted. Scientists have gathered multitudes of DNA and historical evidence indicating that the bacteria was likely the cause of the pandemic and that fleas were the primary vector of transmission. Scientists have not been able to produce reliable evidence in order to disprove the theory and make a case for other ideas.

. . .

## Spread of the Disease

With the acceptance of the Yersinia pestis theory comes the question: how did this disease spread to become the Black Plague? The disease managed to make its way across Asia and Europe. It eventually found its way to North Africa. These areas would experience recurrences of the plague long after the end of the initial pandemic. However, scholars had not been able to determine the origins and path of the disease until recently.

Scientists have traced the initial outbreak back to Mongolia, where a large outbreak spread among the populace in the 1330's. The bacteria is enzootic to a variety of rodents in Asia, specifically in the Central region. The bacteria is believed to have formed somewhere near the border of China and Kyrgyzstan, about one-thousand years before the beginning of the pandemic.

While most scientists agree that the origin of the disease is somewhere in Asia, there are disputes on exactly where that location is. Many claim that China is specifically responsible, while others point to Central Asia or the Middle East. The Plague of Justinian in 541 AD was believed to have been caused by the same bacteria, leading some scholars to claim that the definite origins are Central Asia and that the rodent population simply harbored the bacteria until the time of the Black Death.

Despite the arguments regarding the location of disease origination, almost all scholars agree that at least some of the disease spread happened on a trade route known as the Silk Road. Mongolian groups used this road for both trade purposes and for purposes of war.

The Mongols are particularly blamed for the introduction of Yersinia pestis to Europe due to an event known as the siege of Caffa, which happened in Crimea. A population of Genoese colonies existed in the area, with the one in Caffa consisting primarily of traders. The Mongols attempted to take over the city by force and at one point began throwing plague-ridden corpses into the settlement. The traders of the colony fled by sea, bringing the disease to Sicily and mainland Europe. The crew were all either ill or deceased by the time they reached their destination of Messina, Sicily. Some ships never made it and were found on shorelines, the crews inside all dead from the disease.

The crews—both alive and dead—as well as the ships, all carried the disease. The rats and fleas inside the ships were a particular danger to those who searched the ships that had found their way to shorelines once their crews had all passed on. This looting helped ignite the initial spread across the Italian peninsula, which led to the spread across the rest of the European continent.

The disease spread rapidly. The continent was still reeling from the impact of the Little Ice Age and the

Great Famine. Food was still in short supply and while the famine was technically over, the populace was still underfed and malnourished, leading to weaknesses of the immune system. This led to constant illness and a near constant shortage of workers, leading to more issues with food supply. This cycle was ongoing, with famine leading to illness and illness leading to more famine. Landlords panicked and increased the costs of renting, leading to even more starvation and poverty. This left Europe particularly vulnerable to the disease once it began to spread.

From Italy, the disease spread to France, Portugal, and England. Afterwards, it was found in Scandinavia starting with Norway and then traveling to Bergen, Sweden, and Denmark. Russia was the last European victim to be infected, particularly in the northeast. Afterwards, the spread continued into the Middle East with Egypt, Palestine, Saudi Arabia, Iraq, and Yemen all eventually facing the consequences of the pandemic.

Thus, it is believed that overall, the pandemic began in Asia, where it originally was found in the wild rodent population. Through trade and warfare, the disease spread to Europe where it decimated the population. Eventually, it found its way to North Africa and the Middle East where it continued to take the lives of millions.

## 3. Symptoms and Diagnosis

**Physical Symptoms**

There are three variants of the disease caused by the Yersinia pestis bacteria: the pneumonic plague, the septicemic plague, and the bubonic plague. Each variant infects a different part of the body and leads to different symptoms. In addition, two of the variants are significantly more fatal than the commonly discussed bubonic variant.

The pneumonic plague manifests as an infection of the lungs. It often begins a few days to a week after exposure to the bacteria. Occasionally, one can catch a pneumonic infection after overcoming one of the other two variants. This variant of the disease is always fatal if left untreated. Treatment during the events of the Black Death were not successful and modern treatment requires rigorous courses of antibiotics within twenty-four hours of contracting the disease in order to be most effective.

The pneumonic plague often begins with symptoms that are typical to most respiratory infections. Fever is often the first to develop, followed by weakness and headache. Nausea is also common at this stage. Then pneumonia, an infection of the alveoli in the lungs, quickly begins to develop. This soon leads to difficulty breathing, a cough that may produce blood alongside sputum, and chest pain.

Unlike the other two variants of the plague, the pneumonic plague can be easily spread from person to person. This can lead to a rapid spread in densely populated areas. It is sometimes argued that this form of the plague was likely the primary form found during the Black Death pandemic, but this has not been proven.

The septicemic plague is a dangerous variant of the Black Plague that infects the blood of an individual. This variant is also always fatal if not treated. Unlike the other variants, the septicemic plague can sometimes remain asymptomatic in an individual before causing their death. However, in most cases some symptoms are present long before the individual succumbs to the illness.

The lesser symptoms of the septicemic plague include a variety of uncomfortable maladies including stomach upset, fever, and chills. However, as the plague progresses, the symptoms become significantly more severe. Patients often experience bruising due to issues with blood coagulation, bleeding from various parts of the body, hematemesis (or vomiting blood), breathing problems, and low blood pressure. This soon turns into organ failure, shock, and tissue death. Soon after, the person expires. This variant can also cause blood clots to form throughout the entire body, causing a variety of issues due to blockage on top of the symptoms listed above.

While this version of the plague can be transmitted from person to person, it is not common for this to happen. Instead, the most common method of transmission is via flea bite. Patients are often treated with antibiotics and draining of lymph nodes as necessary. Septicemic plague was not as common as the other two variants during the Black Death; however, it did still kill a large number of people during this time period.

The bubonic plague is the most well-known form of the Black Plague, with pictures of lesion covered peasants plastered on history textbooks all over the world. Despite its popularity, the bubonic plague is the least deadly variant of the Black Plague, with 40-60% of those infected being able to survive despite a lack of treatment. If treated, individuals have a 90% survival rate.

The symptoms of the bubonic plague start a few days to a week after exposure to the bacteria. It often begins with chills, fever, malaise, and muscle cramps. Individuals who have had the disease have compared the beginning to having the flu. Soon, symptoms progress. Individuals may have seizures and may begin experiencing painful lymph nodes. Soon, the lymph nodes will swell and create buboes, which is what the variant is named after as it is the hallmark symptom. Tissue death often follows and individuals may lose extremities, such as toes and fingers, to gangrene.

All three variants ransacked society during the events of the Black Death. The pneumonic plague, manifesting as a respiratory illness that quickly caused severe pneumonia, likely was the most dangerous variant of the Black Death. The bubonic plague, while less dangerous, was the most well-known version with the classic representation of buboes covered bodies being a primary image of the plague. The septicemic plague, while not as common, was equally deadly due to the quick organ failure that resulted from the blood infection. All of them are still found in our modern world, although better hygiene practices and medical care have significantly lowered the risk of transmission and death.

## Medieval Medical Knowledge

Medieval medical knowledge was limited, as many individuals did not even attribute disease to medical conditions. Medical information at the time came from a set of ancient Greek and Roman philosophers and doctors including Hippocrates, Aristotle, and Galen. However, the individuals who studied these texts never actually treated patients. Instead, medicine was practiced by barely trained individuals using what little knowledge they had to try to treat maladies.

Theories of keeping healthy varied by physician, with the concept of "humors" being a common belief during the time of the plague. Healers would tell people that the body contained fluids called "humors" that had to be kept in a proper state of equilibrium. Four of these fluids were identified: black bile, yellow bile, blood, and phlegm. Ingesting pollution in the form of unclean water or unnatural vapors could disrupt this equilibrium, leading to illness. This relates to miasma theory as noxious air was believed to be a primary disruptor of humors.

Once the plague reached France, scholars teaching at the University of Paris furthered this theory by coming up with the idea that planets caused the release of this noxious air. They claimed the conjunction of Mars, Jupiter, and Saturn aligning led to the release of miasma from the Earth which spread via wind. The miasma infected the hearts of the individuals infected with the plague and caused them to fall ill.

However, medical knowledge was sometimes seen as unnecessary. The Roman Catholic church ultimately had control over medicine during this time period and spread the idea that there was nothing to cure. Suffering was seen as part of the experience of being human and disease was an extension of this condition. Deadly diseases, and specifically the Black Death, were labeled as God punishing the sin of the people. Instead of treating the disease in a medical manner, the church organized marching and gatherings where people would pray for the disease to end, leading to further spread. Muslim scholars shared similar beliefs, but instead framed it as an easy path to paradise instead of a punishment. Muslims were encouraged to not try to stop or prevent the plague, as it was sent from God to bring them to martyrdom, and one should never go against God.

Overall, medical knowledge was limited during the time of the Black Death and access to proper physicians had not yet been established. Many medical theories involving the "humors" of the body surrounded the plague, but folkloric beliefs had more of a pronounced presence with miasma theory being one of the most popular ideas spread. The church rejected medical reasonings behind the disease, instead pushing the illness as an act of God. This led to a populace that was fully at the mercy of the plague.

. . .

## Misdiagnosis and Mistaken Beliefs

Some physicians did try to give advice on how one could avoid the plague. The first piece of advice often given was to run from the plague. Individuals were told to flee once it arrived in their community and go to a plague-free location. This only helped to spread the plague via the asymptomatic individuals carrying the disease or bringing along fleas as they fled. They then infected the new locations they chose to reside in. People were also told to avoid doing any strenuous activity and to avoid bathing, leading to further weakening of the immune system. In order to combat the inhalation of plague vapors, people were also encouraged to inhale intense smells, such as those wafting from nearby latrines (a toilet, especially a communal one in a camp or barracks).

Some beliefs were more folkloric than others. Some doctors believed that carrying flowers or burning incense could prevent one from falling ill. Others believed that religious medals and papers containing magical incantations could make an individual immune from the plague or that rubbing onions on buboes (a swollen inflamed lymph node in the armpit or groin) could draw out the toxins causing the disease. One method was particularly jarring. Known as the "Vicary Method," doctors would tie a live chicken to a plague victim with the bird pressed firmly on the patient's buboes. Supposedly, they believed chickens used their rear to breath and thus could breathe the disease out of the victim's wounds. Snakes were another animal used in treatment of the plague. Doctors would cut them up and place the pieces on the wounds of the plague victim, claiming the evil from the snake would draw out the evil from the disease. Con-artists also sold unicorn horn as a potential remedy. They claimed it could only be gathered by a virgin woman, as unicorns will only appear to them. Historians believe that at best, the individuals were selling powdered narwhal tusk or rhinoceros's horn. People would mix the powder with water and drink it.

Other remedies were significantly more dangerous. Bloodletting was a common way of restoring the "humors" in individuals sick with the plague. This was sometimes done with a knife, but often it was done with leeches. Potions including odd ingredients, such as ground chicken bones, were also exceedingly popular cures. Some surgeons advised individuals to cut open their buboes and burn them. Others advised individuals to drink the pus from their wounds. Even more disgusting, some physicians made a sort of salve using various herbs mixed with human feces, which would be placed directly on the inflected buboes and then covered with a cloth bandage.

Some remedies held more weight scientifically, such as that of using Four Thieves Vinegar. The concoction was more of an agent of prevention than a cure, but ultimately it may have actually aided some in avoiding illness. The legend states that a set of four thieves used the potion so that they would not become ill when conducting their robberies at night, specifically when robbing dead plague victims. The potion consisted of vinegar and garlic with various herbs and spices. Vinegar is an antiseptic, meaning that vinegar did aid in killing bacteria that could have caused one to become infected with the plague. However, this has never been proven to have actually occurred. Another potentially helpful preventative was to surround one with fire from torches and fire pits. While this method was costly, impractical, and risked burning, it did have the potential to kill disease via heat. It is not believed that many individuals actually attempted this method, however.

Not all attempts at curing the disease were medical or even folkloric in nature. One attempted remedy was religious in nature and was eventually condemned by the Catholic church. Individuals formed groups with the sole intention of flagellating (flog) themselves in public in an attempt to gain the mercy of God. They used whips with knots and spikes attached in order to purge the sins from their bodies. They would flagellate themselves in bloody displays and fall upon the ground, gaining attention from the public in the process. The church deemed this a form of heresy.

In conclusion, a variety of proposed remedies and preventatives were used during the Black Death. At best, most were useless. Many were dangerous and actually increased the likelihood of illness. A small few had some basis in fact, such as the use of vinegar to disinfect surfaces. However, the impact of these remedies were minimal and ultimately did not make much of a difference in the overall death toll.

## 4. The Impact of the Black Plague

### Death Tolls and Population Decline

Despite the efforts of flagellators and unicorn horn salesmen, the Black Plague caused the populations of Europe, Asia, and Northern Africa to decline drastically. Altogether, it is estimated that anywhere from seventy-five million to two hundred million people died (the world's population was estimated to be around 450 million to 475 million people) during the pandemic across all regions. At least twenty-five million of these deaths were from Europe, killing anywhere from thirty to fifty percent of the population. According to ancient reports, it was said that at least twenty million people died of the disease in Asia. However, this is likely a huge underestimate as Asia had a much larger population than Europe.

This large death toll mirrors previous and later pandemics of the bubonic plague. The Plague of Justinian had ravaged Europe from 541 to 542, killing about twenty-five million people. Initially, it was believed that this plague killed half of Europe, but modern estimates claim that it was likely somewhere close to only one quarter of the population.

After the initial Black Death came the Italian plague in 1629. This resurgence of the black plague killed one million people and ended in 1631. Later, the Great Plague of London would kill one-hundred thousand people in 1665. The Third Plague (around 1855), located in China and India, killed twelve million individuals before it led to the discovery of the Yersinia pestis bacteria. This led to medical advancements which eventually allowed for treatment protocols to be created and also allowed for preventative measures to be utilized.

Today, there are around six hundred and fifty cases of the Black Plague per year. Only ten percent of those who contract the disease die from it due to the availability of medical treatment. While there have been recent outbreaks, such as the 2017 outbreak in Madagascar, the death toll has been minimal. The disease that once killed millions now kills less than one-hundred individuals per year thanks to antibiotics and pest control measures.

Thus, while the disease was initially easily spread, it is no longer common. During the pandemic, it killed large portions of the population, but now the very few individuals who contract it only have a small risk of death due to the advancements that have been made in medicine.

## Social and Economic Consequences

The Black Death drastically changed social life in Europe and the economic system of Europe. Some of these changes, such as individuals becoming more reclusive, were temporary. Other changes, such as the fall of the feudal system, became permanent after the plague ended.

Socially, people began to isolate themselves. While government mandated quarantines were not common during the initial pandemic, individuals often took it upon themselves to avoid interacting with others. People sometimes isolated themselves alongside family in an attempt to remain together and weather the storm of disease. Others, however, chose to abandon their families and friends, uncertain of it was safe to interact with anybody at all. Some families and individuals abandoned their homes, fleeing in attempt to outrun the plague and find a new home that would not fall victim to the decay.

Funerals were no longer a time for gathering and mourning. Areas that still performed religious rites for the dead did the bare minimum necessary and did not encourage anybody to attend the events. In many locations, the bodies were considered to be a large vector of disease and thus, funerals were abandoned altogether. In other locations, the death toll simply climbed too high to engage in such activities. In these locations, bodies either lay rotting in the streets or in large pits dug for the purpose of serving as a mass grave.

While isolation was a common tactic to handling the horrors of the plague, some individuals opted to do the opposite. For many, death was something that they expected to befall them. They saw their family members and community members all succumb to the illness and could not help but feel as if there was minimal hope for survival. These individuals chose not to hide. Instead, they decided to fill their last days with as much fun as possible. These individuals engaged in casual romantic flings and danced the night away, hoping to make their last moments memorable. Later, once the plague had officially come to an end, many more would mimic these actions, celebrating with intimate affairs.

The economy also had a rather intense response to the pandemic. A sudden inflation hit the market due to the scarcity of goods. Farmers and laborers were unable to work due to illness and attempts at quarantine. Trade had become dangerous due to the plague, leading some merchants to cease trading for the time being. Those who continued trading were subjected to quarantines and other regulations which slowed their progress dramatically.

The lack of labor led to an increase in wages. For the first time, serfs (a person who is forced to work on a plot of land) were able to choose who they wanted to work for. If they did not like the pay or conditions provided by one lord, there were several others willing to hire them immediately. Thus, lords had to make working conditions more favorable to laborers and had to increase the amount of pay offered. Despite the drastic increase in the cost of goods, the pay of laborers rose even higher. The class lines began to dissolve as the standard of living increased.

The upper class intended to maintain the class system despite the economic changes. The peasant class, feeling empowered by recent changes, began to revolt. The upper class was determined to secure social power via the use of fancy garments. The lower class legally was forbidden from wearing these clothing items in order to ensure that they did not attempt to pass themselves off as part of the upper class. These laws were called sumptuary laws.

In addition, various leaders created laws that harmed the economy in an attempt to manage the risks associated with the plague. Some kings outlawed the export of food items, instead insisting they be kept for usage by citizens of the community. Governments also began fixing prices on goods in an attempt to ensure that costs were profitable and reasonable. Many leaders began to take an active stance against the usage of black markets, and fishing operations were often forced to shut down. Often, these laws could not be enforced. When they were enforced, it often contributed to the inflation instead of resolving it. Pirates began to loot ships in an attempt to steal grain, leading to further supply issues.

However, towards the end of the pandemic and for years afterwards, the population reduction would prove to be beneficial to those of the lower classes. Peasants would soon be able to afford more food, as there was less of a demand due to the decline in population. In addition, wages increased as laborers were no longer easily available. The labor market became competitive, giving laborers some choice over who they would work for and where they would live. Meat and dairy products became more affordable due to the increase in pasture lands as farmland was left abandoned after the deaths of many farmers. In general, animal farming replaced growing grain as the primary agricultural activity. The activity required much less human labor to produce similar amounts of food.

Attempts to prevent the betterment of daily lives for peasants were common. Prices were sometimes fixed by government officials simply to ensure that peasants could not afford large amounts of goods. Competitive pay was forbidden in England with the passage of the Statute of Laborers 1351. This act prevented laborers from asking for pay above what they made in 1346. A similar law called the Ordinance of Laborers was passed in 1349, causing peasants attempting to relocate from their current work locations to be imprisoned. Despite the passage of these laws, there were minimal attempts to enforce them. The peasant class still managed to benefit greatly from the situation.

Thus, while life initially became more difficult due to the pandemic, it overall had a positive effect on those belonging to the lower class. Labor shortages allowed for negotiation amongst peasants and lords, goods became more affordable, and meat became more accessible. While the upper class attempted to prevent these changes from influencing the role of the lower class, they ultimately failed to reach their goal. The events of the pandemic would eventually lead to the fall of the feudal system.

**Psychological Impact on Survivors**

Although the study of psychology did not begin until five hundred years after the events of the Black Death, modern psychologist have been able to determine the likely impact of the pandemic on the human psyche by analyzing historical records. The pandemic had a traumatic impact on society, with the loneliness of social isolation only furthering the depression many individuals felt during this time. Individuals reacted to these stressors and feelings in a variety of different ways, leading to many expected behaviors and some that are still rather perplexing.

Overall, the plague forced humans to recognize the inherent fragility of their lives. Many individuals handled this newfound feeling by engaging in zealous displays of religious fanaticism, such as the flagellants who whipped themselves in order to try to gain the mercy of God. Towns and villages came together to pray in some instances, an attempt to use community to overcome the fear and loneliness of the situation.

Other individuals, unable to grasp the reality of their situation, lashed out in anger. This anger fueled hatred against many groups. Unable to attack the actual enemy, people chose other humans to stand in as targets for their fear and rage. This led to persecution of many groups including Jews, the Romani people, beggars, lepers, foreigners, homosexuals, and women.

Some individuals instead attempted to express their fears via art. Paintings from the time showcase death and the afterlife as primary themes. Music from the period is embedded with similar concepts.

Modern psychologists believe that most individuals at the time likely suffered from post-traumatic stress disorder, which is caused by experiencing a life-threatening event and not being able to process the situation. For multiple years, individuals lived in fear of death. They watched others die slow, painful death due to disease and famine. They walked streets that were covered in dead bodies, and the smell of decay often permeated their homes. There was no happy ending either as most who died were tossed into burial pits instead of being given proper funeral rights. These experiences combined left people feeling as if they were in a constant state of danger and likely persisted long after the plague ended.

Depression was also an ailment at the time. Individuals often isolated themselves—whether by force or by voluntary choice. Humans are a social species and isolation is difficult for humans to handle. Many individuals likely felt alone and hopeless during these periods of quarantine, leading to worsening mental health.

One interesting phenomenon that manifested during the time of the Black Plague was called "Dancing Mania." Essentially, some individuals handled the stress of the pandemic by dancing. This is a common way that communities sometimes process difficult events. However, while some individuals danced and then went about their normal lives, others literally danced themselves to death. Individuals would sometimes dance until they entered an odd trance, until they passed out, or until they died from exhaustion. While there is no official consensus on the cause of this dancing, it is believed to have been a trauma response due to the stress of the plague.

Overall, the situation likely had a negative impact on the mental health of medieval society. Individuals felt alone and helpless, leading to psychological distress. This distress manifested in a variety of ways, some of which were unhealthy and harmful. Some methods, such as dancing until one physically could not dance any longer, even led to death.

## 5. Responses to the Black Plague

**Religious Responses**

People became extremely religious in the early days of the plague, praying for God to save them. The Christian population believed that some grave sin must be the cause of the illness sweeping across the continent.

Many blamed the Jews, claiming that heresy was the sin that led to God's wrath in the form of buboes and decay. Jewish communities became a huge target of Christian violence. Some Jewish settlements, such as Mainz and Cologne, were completely destroyed during this time period due to the accusations against Jews.

Other Christians condemned the lepers, stating that it must be their uncleanliness that upset the divine father. Many individuals also blamed foreigners in general, stating that they too were not hygienic. The Romani people were also scapegoats and were often accused of somehow causing the pandemic on purpose. However, the one sin that gained the most scrutiny at the time was one of the flesh: lust.

Many scholars and religious officials specifically blamed homosexuals for the plague. Some well-known figures that held this opinion were Thomas Brinton, the Bishop of Rochester, and Bernardino of Siena, a famous Franciscan missionary. Bernardino specifically believed the participation in such acts by young boys was what caused the Black Death, even mentioning that their tights were too revealing and that alone was sinful.

These declarations caused a fear of homosexuality to arise in cities such as Florence, Italy. Many alleged homosexuals faced brutal punishment, including execution. One of the youngest victims of these executions was a fifteen-year-old boy named Giovanni di Giovanni. He was forced to ride throughout the city on the back of a donkey, then he was mutilated publicly. It is believed this public act of violence was meant to deter others from committing homosexual acts.

The church as a whole, however, did not directly point the blame towards homosexuality. Instead, they claimed that all sexual acts were likely the cause of God's wrath. It did not matter who engaged in the activity. It was the sheer fact that society had become morally scandalous that led to the pandemic. Form fitting and revealing clothing was a specific evil that the church hated and blamed for the disease. Even shoes were considered to be sensual in nature, with long, pointed toes being a major concern to some of the clergy.

Many individuals engaged in constant prayer and others even engaged in self-flagellation in an attempt to appease God. Groups of individuals known as flagellants would walk from one town to another in order to share their gospel and their suffering. They would strip down to the waist in order to publicly whip themselves. Once bloodied, they would call for all of the witnesses to repent.

Witnesses would often fall into a frenzy over the display. The flagellants would pray and the public would beg for forgiveness. Everyone would watch as they whipped themselves and some would fall over in gratitude. The blood of the flagellants was sometimes collected on handkerchiefs and clothes, which people believed could ward off the plague. Ironically, this only furthered the spread of the disease.

Some Christians began to blame the Jewish population for the disease, leading to several groups hunting down Jewish individuals and torturing them. They claimed that the Jews were poisoning local wells, a claim that was made more believable due to the Jews avoidance of communal waters. Many historical records state that the Jewish populace seemed to fall ill less often, further inciting the anger of Christians. Modern scientists believe that this could be due to the rules regarding cleanliness that Jewish populations are expected to follow. These hygiene practices could have helped prevent the spread of the plague, inciting the wrath of populations who were stricken with disease.

The church decreed that the Jewish population was not to blame for the plague. They ordered that Christians should not persecute the Jewish populations. Christians often ignored these orders. In a similar manner, flagellation was declared as heresy. Once again, these declarations were often ignored. Due to the failure of prayer in preventing the spread of illness and death, religion decreased in popularity towards the end of the pandemic.

The clergy preached gospels of tribulation and victory over illness, only for them to succumb to the illness as well. This is partially due to the sick seeking out aid by finding monasteries in order to ask the clergy there for help. Many clergy members died due to this and were later replaced by poorly trained individuals who had only undergone the most minimal of training. This shortage also gave women more opportunities to serve actively in their congregations, as male participants could not always be found.

Meanwhile, religion thrived in Muslim communities during this time. The suffering brought by the plague was deemed a way for one to achieve martyrdom. Muslims were encouraged to go about their lives as usual and to make no attempt to avoid the disease. They believed that the disease—despite the horrors that it often brought—was ultimately a gift. It was thought that God was bestowing upon them an easy path to paradise. Muslim scholars declared attempts to avoid contracting the illness were attempts to avoid God's will and his gift. These beliefs carried the Muslim population throughout the entirety of the plague. While the Christian population lost faith, the Muslims affected by the pandemic only grew stronger in their faith.

However, some Muslims did not accept this idea. A small group of Muslims argued that the plague was likely a punishment from God due to the sin of fornication. In communities where this theory was accepted, men often blamed women for the pandemic. In Cairo, Egypt, for example, women were not allowed to travel in public during the plague. It was believed that doing so risked causing men to commit the sin of lust. Eventually, this ban was lifted as it inhibited female servants from completing their assigned duties.

Overall, the pandemic resulted in a sudden rise in religious extremism and then a decline in religious beliefs. Individuals attempted to seek forgiveness and protection from God, only to see the clergy themselves fall victim to the disease. Various groups were targeted for their sins, with several groups including homosexuals and Jews being subjected to great violence in the name of God. Muslims, on the other hand, overall accepted the plague as God's will and remained strong in their faith throughout the pandemic.

## Quarantine Measures

One of the few helpful measures taken during the Black Death was that of quarantine. Some physicians and scholars recommended that individuals, especially those who were ill, should stay away from others during the pandemic. This became a mandated procedure in the city of Dubrovnik, located in Croatia. At the time, the area was known as Ragusa and was part of Dalmatia. The city was a bustling trade city and was renowned for its wealth. It wanted to protect its status, but could not afford to simply shut down the area as larger cities often did during the pandemic. Instead, they had to find a way to allow trade to continue without risking infection from the plague.

The state declared that any individuals wishing to enter the city would need to first isolate themselves in special, unpopulated locations before they could be deemed safe enough to allow them entry. This lasted thirty days and took place on neighboring islands in various leftover buildings, with isolated individuals all having scribes, guards, gravediggers, and cleaners available to them. This ensured anybody infected with the plague would either be healed or dead by the end of the waiting period. Those who survived were allowed entry. However, this was only effective to some degree as the plague could last as long as thirty-seven days in some individuals before they died.

Eventually, the Venetian Senate proposed a change to the length of isolation, making it forty days and effectively creating a system to prevent plague-infected visitors from entering the city-state. The change in time was based on biblical cannon, where many important events lasted approximately forty days, such as Jesus' time in the desert and the great flood that God had sent to destroy the wicked. This is also where the term "quarantine" originates from as it references the Italian word for forty, which is *quaranta*. Individuals who chose to forgo the waiting period were punished via torture and removal of the extremities.

Eventually, the original improvised system would be improved by the creation of Lazarettos, which were large stone buildings with cells for individuals to isolate in. They had windows allowing them to view the outside world. In addition, tools would eventually be invented that eased the struggle of maintaining this isolation. Examples include long sticks or poles with pointed ends that allowed guards to encourage distance between individuals, as well as desks with special holes carved into them in order to allow for contactless payment.

Around the time the Lazarettos were built, other cities had begun quarantining as well. This would take place during the Second Pandemic. In 1636, London and Westminster in England joined Dalmatia in their attempts to promote quarantine. The government claimed that quarantine was an effective preventative measure against the plague, yet many historical records dispute this claim and show evidence that the government utilized this isolation as a punishment.

Implementation of the quarantine policy varied by church parish. Some individuals noticed that class had a large influence over whether or not individuals were forced to quarantine, and some considered it a direct punishment on lower class individuals. The wealthy all were allowed to flee the area and move elsewhere before the policy was officially put into place. The peasants, unable to simply pack up and move, were forced to stay in the area and adhere to the quarantine instructions.

In some instances, the quarantine was village-based. While neighbors were allowed to go about their business and even socialize amongst each other, outsiders were forbidden to enter the village. In other situations, individuals were the ones quarantined, either by being forced to remain at home or by being moved to special asylums called "pest houses," which were often formerly used as leper asylums.

For individuals forced to remain at home, government officials would provide them with food. Special officials were chosen to act as searchers. These individuals would scour the area at night, searching for anybody who may have succumbed to the disease. If a body was found, they would be brought to a mass grave in the middle of the night for burial.

During these times of quarantine, the poor and those foreign to the area were most at risk for being punished if they failed to comply. The state was not shy in expressing its belief that the lower class and those from other lands could be a source of noxious air, directly causing the plague. In addition, those who were forced to quarantine were often locked inside with the rats and fleas that caused the plague, leading some to an inescapable demise.

Overall, quarantine was effective, but controversial. The spread of the plague slowed in areas that adhered to some form of isolation and travel restriction. However, those of the lower class failed to see the benefits of the situation as many slowed died trapped in their houses and in special asylums.

Overall, quarantines were not popularized until the Second Pandemic. Only the city of Ragusa used the practice during the Black Death, forcing traders attempting to enter the city to first isolate themselves. During the Second Pandemic, governments would attempt to force individuals and entire cities to quarantine, but would rarely enforce the policy. The lower class was often the only class affected as the upper class would often flee before the policy could be implemented.

## Cultural Responses and Artistic Expressions

The Black Death caused a massive shift in culture and art during the late medieval period. Death and decay were suddenly the themes of every paining and society grew attached to the morbid and macabre. The overall tone was pessimistic, and often it was clear that artists at the time were attempting to represent an apocalyptic scenario in their works.

The "dance of death" became a recurring image in art pieces and showed skeletons undertaking various actions. Not all of these pieces were graphic in nature, but some artists chose to create gruesome and grisly scenes. Some scenes depicted multiple skeletons, showing the sheer amount of death the pandemic had brought. Some paired skeletons with living humans, attempting to showcase the connection between life and death. All of these art pieces, however, ensured the skeleton was an active participant in whatever was happening in the piece. The skeleton was never an inanimate object, but a living creature that impacted the world around them. One artist that is known for such works is an

Italian named Giacomo Borlone de Burchis, who included many depictions of living skeletons and deceased humans in his paintings.

Other pieces referenced death without the usage of skeletons. Some pieces, such as the painting *The Chronicles of Gilles Li Muisis* located in the monastery of St. Martin the Righteous, instead choose to portray death via the medium of coffins and dead bodies. In this painting, you see a small group of people carrying the coffin of a loved one, each with a look of intense emotion on their faces. Pieces such as these belong to a category called "Memento Mori," which exists to remind humans of their own mortality.

Other themes that were common in art were usually of a religious nature. The devil could often be seen in paintings, guiding individuals towards sin, death, and illness. Sometimes, the Virgin Mary and various Saints would make an appearance, hinting towards forgiveness and deliverance from disease.

Some non-religious themes that could also be found in late medieval art included various doctor-related motifs. Many outlandish remedies are depicted in these works, such as bloodletting and the uses of various salves. Sometimes, doctors are purposefully depicted as being unintelligent, as if to show their ineffectiveness.

Art during the time period of the Black Death revolved around concepts that everyone feared and hoped for. Death was the primary theme, exemplified in both the "Memento Mori" and the "Dance of Death" motifs. Healing and hope were sometimes displayed via religious art and depictions of doctors attempting to heal patients. Occasionally, doctor-related art was used to mock the failures of the doctors during this period.

## 6. Later Outbreaks and Legacy

**Recurrence of the Plague**

Despite the initial plague ending around 1351, the lingering bacteria of Yersinia pestis remained in the bodies of rodents and fleas. The Black Death was followed by a series of similar plagues that lasted from the 14th century to the 17th century. Individual cases were found each year during this time period, with some years having a full recurrence of the disease. These instances were referred to collectively as the Second Pandemic. During this period, the plague was what would later be named an endemic.

It is during this Second Pandemic that certain plague-related motifs were created. Plague doctors began to treat patients and appear in artwork during this period. In addition, quarantine became a popular way to manage the spread of disease, a concept that was only used in Ragusa, Dalmatia, during the initial pandemic.

During the Second Pandemic, individuals did not treat the disease as a great event as with the first pandemic. Instead, the disease was an ongoing part of daily life. Many individuals still died, but ultimately people only panicked during large outbreaks. It was during these outbreaks that quarantines would often take place.

Eventually, another plague pandemic ravaged Asia from 1855-1859. Hong Kong faced a large amount of death from this pandemic, with over two-thousand individuals dying in two months during the Hong Kong plague. The city of Canton had one of the largest death tolls overall, with 80,000 dying by June 1984. During this time, immigrants spread the disease to the United States, although it did not do nearly as much damage there as it did in Asia. It was also during this pandemic that a scientist, Alexandre Yersin, was finally able to identify the bacteria that caused the plague.

Alexandre Emile Jean Yersin (22 September 1863 – 1 March 1943) was a Swiss-French physician and bacteriologist. He is remembered as the co-discoverer of the bacillus responsible for the bubonic plague or pest, which was later named in his honour: Yersinia pestis.

Modern instances of the plague are relatively rare. One of the most modern instances of a multi-person outbreak happened in Madagascar in 2017. This outbreak killed 170 people, but infected thousands more. The plague is still found in rodents around the world, but cases still remain uncommon. However, scientists fear that one day the bacteria may become resistant to antibiotics, which would allow for another large-scale pandemic to take hold.

The plague has been a continuous part of human history since the Black Death. The Second Pandemic continued for hundreds of years and created a lot of the imagery we associate with plagues. A third plague later led to the discovery of the bacteria that eventually would lead to medical advancements creating an effective treatment protocol. While occasional outbreaks do still happen, death from the disease is now uncommon.

## Impact on Public Health and Medicine

The Black Death led to medicine taking a more direct approach in the study of the body. Medicine became less about philosophy and more about practical methods of treatment. Physicians, who had been proven to be unable to treat the disease, had to work to prove themselves worthy of their status as medical practitioners. This led to some tension between surgeons, who actively practiced medicine, and the physicians who were essentially scholars at the time. This divergence influenced the trajectory of medicine heading towards actual disease treatment and prevention, as opposed to just understanding the human condition.

Modern medicine has led to most cases of the plague being resolved relatively quickly. The mortality rate is now around ten percent, with most individuals responding well to antibiotics. Individuals can be easily tested for the Yersinia pestis bacteria via samples of blood, sputum, and fluids from lymph nodes if there is a reason to suspect plague infection.

Those who test positive are often given a series of antibiotics intravenously. This treatment lasts approximately two weeks. The following antibiotics may be used for this purpose: gentamicin, doxycycline, ciprofloxacin, levofloxacin, moxifloxacin, and chloramphenicol. However, some forms of the plague are now becoming antibiotic-resistant, leading to concerns of potential future resurgences of the disease.

There are now vaccinations that can be used to help prevent infections of Yersinia pestis. However, there have been minimal studies done to test the effectiveness of the vaccine. Those that have been done show that the vaccine decreases the likelihood of contracting the disease and lessens the severity of the disease if contracted, however, it does not totally prevent contracting the illness. The vaccine is also only recommended for a small number of individuals. These include individuals who work with the Yersinia pestis bacteria or with animals that harbor the bacteria, as well as those working in disaster areas where the disease is prevalent among the animal population. Other groups eligible for vaccine access may include individuals working in enzootic plague areas where preventing exposure to rodents and fleas is challenging, and individuals in occupations that entail contact with infected rodents.

Overall, the events of the Black Plague forced physicians to take a more direct approach in their study of the human body. Doctors began to focus on actually treating and curing illnesses, leading to the modern practices we see today. In addition, the plague is now overall considered treatable, with antibiotics being the primary course of treatment. Vaccines are also available to reduce the risk of transmission to individuals who qualify.

## Historical Significance and Legacy of the Black Plague

Historically, the Black Plague is one of the defining moments in human history. All modern diseases and pandemics are compared to the Great Pestilence that ransacked Europe in the 1340's. It is still considered the worst pandemic in human history, killing over twenty-five million people in Europe alone. Everything associated with death and the macabre borrows from the imagery of the plague, with skeletons and plague doctors being visible on many pieces of modern artwork.

The plague is also still credited with bringing about the end of the feudal system in Europe. Due to labor shortages, the peasants were able to negotiate for better pay and conditions. The class system began to fall apart, and eventually feudalism gave way to capitalism, which is still the primary economic system of many western countries.

In addition, the plague caused the Roman Catholic Church to lose many followers. This allowed more freedom of thought and less dependence on the church. Eventually, this led to the Italian Renaissance, where art and science began to flourish.

Modern media still uses the Black Death as inspiration. Its legacy lives on not only in history books, but in video games such as the *Assassin's Creed* series and in music such as the album *Prequelle* by the band Ghost.

Truly, the way that the Black Death changed the course of humanity is remarkable. Through death and illness came great economic and social freedom for the lower class. In addition, the imagery from the plague is still utilized today to express themes of death and decay.

# 7. Conclusion

## Final Thoughts

The Black Death is one of the darkest chapters of human history, showing the lunacy that panic can cause and also revealing the fragile veil between life and death. When humans have no where to turn, they will act erratically in an attempt to escape a foe that is not tangible.

The disease itself is frightening. It can infect your body via the lungs, the blood, or the lymph nodes. Without treatment, at least half of humans who contract it will die. The only reason humanity is not still isolating and hiding from this illness is due to the existence of antibiotics.

Despite the pain and suffering of the pandemic, humanity managed to utilize it for the betterment of society. The lower class used the labor shortages to negotiate for better working conditions, eventually leading to the fall of feudalism which had kept a majority of the western world in poverty. Physicians used their failures to propel them into a more practical study of medicine, leading to the modern medicine we have now.

Truly, despite the hardships and evils that the plague brought to humanity, it also left it with the gifts of self-awareness, resilience, and willingness to change. Without the plague, it is possible we would still be stuck in the dark ages, unable to treat even the most rudimentary ailments.

## Lessons Learned from the Black Plague

Ultimately, the Black Plague has taught us that individuals will always seek answers to whatever befalls them, even if it means accepting something without having any true evidence. Human innovation as well as lunacy is inspired by events such as the Black Death pandemic. When no cure is available and the science needed to find one is not there, individuals will resort to folklore, religious fanaticism, and rudimentary experimentation in order to soothe their concerns.

Despite this, sometimes these dark times lead to bright futures. Such events can push tensions until they break, leading to upheavals of social expectations and a newfound strength within a population. It can take power away from institutions that are abusing the populace, such as lords and corrupted church officials, and give it back to the society.

Suffering also increases the importance and significance of the arts, leading to fantastic innovations in literature, visual arts, and music. Even the darkest of times create a nostalgic feeling and a desire to recreate the imagery of those somber moments. Thus, even the most horrific events can inspire beautiful works of art.

Science also benefits from these dark events as it drives the desire to uncover the truth behind such frightening happenings and diseases, aiming to prevent their recurrence. Failures to halt such tragedies can prompt a change in technique, ultimately resulting in saving more lives in the future. The inability to alter the present often paves the way for a future filled with well-researched and informed decisions.

Overall, humanity is resilient. We do learn from our mistakes and our failures. Our species truly is able to find the smallest light in the darkness and use it to illuminate the room.

## Bonus!

Thanks for supporting me and purchasing this book! I'd like to send you some freebies. They include:

- The digital version of *500 World War I & II Facts*

- The digital version of *101 Idioms and Phrases*

- The audiobook for my best seller *1144 Random Facts*

Scan the QR code below, enter your email and I'll send you all the files. Happy reading!

# Check out my other books!

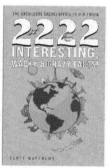

Made in the USA
Columbia, SC
29 January 2024

31121402R00035